GYMNASTICS

BALANCE BEAM

Tips, Rules, and Legendary Stars

by Heather E. Schwartz

Consultant:
Paige Roth
Region IV Xcel Chair
USA Gymnastics Women's Program
Owner Iowa Gym-Nest

CAPSTONE PRESS
a capstone imprint

Snap Books are published by Capstone Press,
1710 Roe Crest Drive, North Mankato, Minnesota 56003
www.mycapstone.com

Library of Congress Cataloging-in-Publication Data
Names: Schwartz, Heather E., author.
Title: Balance beam : tips, rules, and legendary stars / by Heather E. Schwartz.
Description: North Mankato, Minnesota : Capstone Press, 2017 | Series: Snap
    books. Gymnastics | Includes bibliographical references and index.
Identifiers: LCCN 2016001754| ISBN 9781515722229 (library binding) |
    ISBN 9781515722274 (ebook (pdf))
Subjects: LCSH: Balance beam—Juvenile literature.
Classification: LCC GV512 .S34 2017 | DDC 796.44/2—dc23
LC record available at http://lccn.loc.gov/2016001754

Editorial Credits
Gena Chester, editor
Bobbie Nuytten, designer
Kelly Garvin, media researcher
Tori Abraham, production specialist

Image Credits
Alamy Images/SPUTNIK, 21; Capstone Press: Karon Dubke, 1, 8-9 (bottom),
10, 11, 12, 13, 16, 19 (top), 22, Martin Bustamante, 14, 15; iStockphoto/
Brian McEntire, 6; Newscom: Angelo Cozzi Mondadori, 5, Jeff Siner/MCT,
28, Khalilov Yakov Itar-Tass Photos, 26, Paul Kitagaki Jr./MCT, 27, Yang
Zongyou Xinhua News Agency, 29; Shutterstock: 4Max, 15 (bottom), Aspen
Photo, 17, 18, 23, 25, bikeriderlondon, cover, Jiang Dao Hua, 9 (top), Luigi
Fardella, 24, prapass, 22, stefanolunardi, 19 (b), versh, 7

Artistic Elements: Shutterstock: alexdndz, Hakki Arslan, Ludvig

Special Thanks
Thank you to the coaches and gymnasts at GK Gymnastics.

Printed in the United States of America in North Mankato, Minnesota.
009686F16

Table of Contents

Making History
on the Balance Beam

At the 1976 Olympics, 14-year-old gymnast Nadia Comaneci performed a flawless **routine** on the balance beam. She'd already earned a perfect score on the uneven bars. Now she had another 10.0 score from the judges. That day she made history. She was the first woman ever to earn a perfect score in Olympic gymnastics.

Nadia inspired a new generation of young athletes. Girls all over the world were eager to try gymnastics, including the balance beam.

The balance beam is just as exciting and challenging for gymnasts today as it was when Nadia performed. It takes training and practice to nail the event.

Fast Fact:
The balance beam event falls under the category of artistic gymnastics. Other types of gymnastics include rhythmic, trampoline, and sports acrobatics.

routine—a combination of skills performed in a gymnastics event

Nadia Comaneci competed for her home country of Romania in the 1976 Olympics.

Exclusive Events

Only women compete in balance beam. Along with that event, they perform in uneven bars, vault, and floor exercise. Men compete in vault and floor exercise as well. But they also have their own events. Pommel horse, parallel bars, high bar, and rings are events performed only by men. Overall, women compete in four events while men compete in six.

CHAPTER 1

Balance Beam
Basics

Gymnasts performing on the balance beam do jumps, poses, and other skills. It's very similar to other gymnastic events. There is one major difference, though. In balance beam, everything happens on a long, narrow plank. Challenging? Definitely!

Join the Club

Want to try the balance beam event? You need a place to practice, the right equipment, and qualified coaches. You can find them all at a gymnastics club.

USA Gymnastics is an organization that sets rules and runs programs for the sport in the United States. Member clubs must meet USA Gymnastics standards. You can find affiliated clubs near you on the USA Gymnastics official website.

Safety

Safety is a top priority in all gymnastics events. When performing on the beam, staying safe starts with the set-up. A regulation balance beam is constructed of a metal frame covered by a layer of foam and leather. The height can be adjusted for younger gymnasts.

Mats are placed around the beam to cushion gymnasts in case they fall. Coaches and **spotters** are always nearby to help.

spotter—a person who keeps watch to help prevent injury

Fast Fact:
The balance beam used at the Olympics is 4 inches (10 centimeters) wide and 16.4 feet (5 meters) long. It is 4.1 feet (1.2 m) high.

16.4 feet (5 m) long

4 inches (10 cm) wide

4.1 feet (1.2 m) high

Getting Started

Beginning gymnasts perfect their moves on the floor first. Learning skills on the floor helps gymnasts build confidence, strength, and technique. When they jump, turn, and flip through the air, they can use a line of tape on the mat and pretend it is a balance beam. On the mat, they can do this without fear. They don't have to worry about falling off the beam.

When gymnasts are ready, their coaches and trainers help them take their moves from the floor to the beam. They don't have to head straight for a high balance beam. There are lower beams available for practice. Lower beams give gymnasts even more time to build confidence and skills. They can progress from using practice equipment to working on a high balance beam.

Fast Fact:
Low balance beams are 4 inches (10 cm) wide just like high beams. Some lie right on the ground. Others are 6 to 7 inches (15 to 18 cm) off the ground.

What to Wear

Gymnasts can't train in bulky, stiff, street clothes. They need to move and bend easily and comfortably. But their clothing can't be too baggy. Otherwise, coaches won't be able to tell if the gymnasts are in the right positions.

Most female gymnasts wear a leotard to train. Leotards are fitted and also very stretchy. Gymnasts usually go barefoot, but sometimes wear special gymnastics shoes. Socks and other kinds of shoes are too slippery to be safe.

CHAPTER 2
Tricks
to Try

Once your coach decides you're ready, there are plenty of tricks to try out on the high beam. You start with learning **mounts** and basic skills before moving on to more advanced moves.

Mounting the Beam

Moves look amazing on a regulation high beam. Before gymnasts try these moves, they have to mount the balance beam. Scrambling up awkwardly certainly won't impress anyone. But mounting the beam doesn't have to be complicated either. Basic mounts work just as well as more difficult mounts.

Front Support Mount

Stand facing the side of the beam. Put your palms on the beam and grip the far edge with your fingers. Push down and jump up, extending one leg over so you arrive straddling the beam.

mount—to get up on the balance beam or other gymnastics apparatus

10

Leg Swing Mount with Half Turn

Stand parallel to the beam on your left side. Step your left foot forward and place your left arm on the beam. Swing your right leg forward and up over the beam. At the same time, twist your body 180 degrees, so both hands are on the beam. You will arrive straddling the beam in the opposite direction from where you began.

Dismounts

The dismount is just as important as the mount. In competition, it's even more important because it's the last move judges see. Gymnasts perform jumps, twists, and flips as they dismount the beam. When they land, they have to stick it. That means they have to land on their feet with no extra steps once they hit the mat.

Forward Walk

Stand on the beam with your hands on your hips. As you step forward, keep your knees straight. Swing your foot slightly out to the side of the beam. Point your toe and place it on the beam in front of you.

Relevé Walk

Stand on the beam with your hands on your hips. Lift your heels so you are up on your toes. As you step forward, keep your knees straight. Place your foot directly in front of you onto the beam.

Fast Fact:
Relevé is French for "raised." Gymnasts and dancers use this word to describe raising their heels.

Stretching

You need more than strength to perform well on the beam. You also need **flexibility**. You can build flexibility by doing stretches at home and in the gym. A hurdle stretch works the muscles at the back of your thigh. This basic stretch is one that every gymnast should do regularly. Here's how to do it.

1. Warm up your muscles with 10 to 15 minutes of **cardiovascular** exercise, like walking or jogging.

2. Sit with one leg extended in front of you. The other should be bent with your foot on your thigh and your knee pointing out. Point your toes and reach up with your arms as high as you can.

3. Lean forward, keeping your back straight and stomach tight. Go as low as you can while keeping the correct position.

4. Hold for 10 to 15 seconds. Then lift back up so your arms are reaching high again. Flex your toes.

5. Repeat two to three times and switch legs.

flexibility—the ability to bend or move easily
cardiovascular—relating to the heart and blood vessels

Backward Walk

Stand on the beam with your hands on your hips. Keep your knees straight as you step backward. Swing your foot slightly out to the side of the beam. Feel for the top of the beam with your toes. When you find it, place your foot down and continue.

More Advanced Moves

As gymnasts gain experience, they can perform impressive and stylish skills on the balance beam. They can even go airborne!

Handstand

Look down at the beam as you step forward and bend at the waist. Place your hands on the beam, keeping your arms straight. Keeping your legs straight, kick them up and together.

Wolf Jump

Swing your arms to create momentum and jump straight up. While in the air, bend one leg under your body. Stretch the other straight in front of you.

Front Aerial

Push off with one leg while kicking the other behind you.
Arching your back, flip forward and land feet first on the beam.

Fast Fact:
Gymnasts dust chalk on their hands and legs to get a better grip on equipment. The powdered substance absorbs sweat.

CHAPTER 3

Meet to Compete

Gymnastics competitions, or **meets**, give gymnasts a chance to challenge themselves. They can reach for new goals and even win medals. USA Gymnastics runs competitions for gymnasts from beginners to **elite** athletes.

Gymnasts can start in the organization's Junior Olympics as young as 4 years old. If they stick with the sport for years, they can advance through numbered levels of competition. With each level, gymnasts gain experience and skills. Eventually they may compete as elite athletes. In elite programs, gymnasts train for competitions such as the USA Championships, the World Championships, the Pan American Games, and the Olympic Games.

Gymnasts have their performance scored in competition. Judges use a rule book called a Code of Points. When judging gymnasts on beam, they look at form, height of aerial moves, and execution of moves. They note the **artistry** in the routine.

In the Junior Olympic program, a 10.0 is the highest score possible. That used to be true at the elite level too. A new system at the elite level gives gymnasts one score for the difficulty of their routine. A second score deducts points for mistakes in execution. The scores are combined for a final score.

meet—a gymnastics competition that features many events

elite—describes gymnasts who are among the best in the club

artistry—creative skill

Pulling it All Together

Gymnasts who plan to compete string several balance beam moves together into a routine. Balance beam routines are generally about 70 to 90 seconds long. It doesn't sound like much time. So every moment is critical. Judges watch to make sure gymnasts don't go over the time limit.

Putting together a great routine is a balancing act. Gymnasts need to include skills they know they can perform well. They also need to include moves that will impress judges and earn a high score.

Where should you turn when you're eager to compete? Your coach, of course! He or she can help you plan a routine that will showcase your skills and meet the requirements for your level of competition.

Pack Your Gym Bag

Don't leave home for competition without critical items that will get you through the event.
Be sure to bring:

- healthy snacks
- a water bottle
- deodorant
- any equipment you need to protect against injury, such as wrist guards or athletic tape
- hair spray, gel, bands, etc. to keep hair tightly pulled back into a bun or braid
- a jacket and gym pants to stay warm while waiting to perform

Fast Fact:
USA Gymnastics requires long hair to be pulled back and off your face during competition. Some coaches may have additional rules about the types of clips you're allowed to use and even the color of hair bands. Be sure to check rules ahead of time.

Performance Technique

The world's best gymnasts go beyond displaying their technical skill in competition. They **choreograph** balance beam routines that show style and artistry to present themselves as talented performers as well as accomplished athletes. Fifteen-year-old Oksana Omelianchik won a gold medal at the 1985 European Championships with a performance that was practically flawless and fun to watch. Here's why.

- She used the whole beam. Poses and positions are important, but Oksana performed many moves that took her back and forth across the beam too.

- She varied her skills throughout the routine. She mixed up moves to perform poses, then flips, then poses, and then leaps. The variety created a fast-paced routine. She didn't give her audience a chance get bored.

- She included both easier and more difficult skills in her routine. It was challenging, but not so much that it caused her a lot of stress.

- Instead of looking tense or worried, she appeared to be relaxed, confident, and enjoying herself. The audience could relax and enjoy the performance too.

choreograph—to create and arrange movements that make up a routine

Oksana Omelianchik was only 15 years old when she competed at the 1985 European Championships.

CHAPTER 4

Practice
Makes Perfect

Gymnasts often train for years before deciding to compete. When you're preparing for a meet, be sure to take your time. USA Gymnastics recommends gymnasts practice the routine they plan to perform for at least six weeks. However, the amount of time you spend training for a competition is usually up to your coach. He or she can help you create a schedule and make sure you are prepared to compete.

The last week before competition is a good time to perfect your moves. You can also practice exactly what you will experience in competition. For example, you might want to wear a number while you practice. You could try warming up for a timed period that will match the time allowed at the meet.

Practice will help you feel much more comfortable when it's competition day. Working closely with your coach as you train and prepare will help relieve stress too.

See Yourself Succeed

A great deal of focus is put on physical preparation before a meet. But there's plenty a gymnast can do to prepare mentally for a meet as well. **Visualization** helps many gymnasts ease anxiety. Here's how it works. Run through your routine in your mind. Focus carefully on each move you plan to perform, and then imagine yourself performing them perfectly. See yourself earning a high score. Allow yourself to feel happy and proud. Visualization can build your confidence and help you relax, which makes you more likely to succeed.

Positive thinking helps in a similar way. Be your own cheerleader. Replace negative thoughts with positive ones. Tell yourself you can do it.

Eating healthy foods and getting enough sleep helps you prepare both physically and mentally. You need energy and rest in order to perform well, but you also need these things to handle the stress of competition.

visualization—the act of imagining or forming a mental picture

CHAPTER 5

Balance Beam

Legends

Nadia Comaneci and Oksana Omelianchik are not the only gymnastics legends to leave their mark on the balance beam. Gymnasts throughout history and around the world have shaped what it means to perform in the event.

Olga Korbut

In 1969 at the Soviet Union's national championships, Olga Korbut was the first gymnast to perform a backward aerial somersault on the balance beam.

Olga won a gold medal in balance beam for the Soviet Union at the 1972 Olympic Games. She won a silver medal in balance beam at the 1976 Games. She is best known, however, for her originality in gymnastics. Performing new moves, like the backward aerial somersault on the beam, influenced athletes and judges to think differently about what gymnasts can accomplish in the sport.

Beijing 2008 ⠕⠕⠕⠕⠕

Shawn Johnson

Shawn Johnson started doing gymnastics when she was 3 years old. She trained for the Olympics for years. But while practicing on the beam at the 2008 Games, her routine didn't go so well. She just couldn't get it right.

When her big moment came, her training kicked in. She impressed the judges with her strength and confidence as well as her ability to perform a difficult dismount. At age 16 she took home an Olympic gold medal for the United States and became known throughout the world as a champion.

Deng Linlin

Deng Linlin started gymnastics when she was 5 years old. She trained hard for years. At times family members wanted her to quit or at least ease up. But Deng did not want to stop.

In 2012 she competed at the London Olympic Games. She fell while performing on the balance beam in a team event. Her mistake cost her team a medal.

A few days later, she had a chance to redeem herself. She performed on the beam as an individual athlete. Her routine included front flips, back flips, aerials, and difficult leaps. This time she impressed the judges and took home an Olympic gold medal for China.

Simone Biles

Simone Biles started gymnastics at age 6 and worked hard, training and competing for many years. By age 18, she was practicing at least 32 hours each week.

In 2015 she made history in her sport. She became the first woman ever to win three all-around world titles in gymnastics in a row. She had 10 World Championship gold medals in total, including two for balance beam.

Fast Fact:
Women couldn't win individual medals in Olympic gymnastics until 1952.

Becoming a legend on the balance beam takes strength, style, and a great deal of determination. And just like you, these legendary gymnasts all started with learning the basics. Practice and hard work will bring you closer to achieving your gymnastics dreams.

GLOSSARY

artistry (AR-tis-tree)—creative skill

cardiovascular (kahr-dee-oh-VAS-kew-lahr)—relating to the heart and blood vessels

choreograph (KOR-ee-oh-graf)—to create and arrange movements that make up a routine

elite (i-LEET)—describes gymnasts who are among the best in the club

flexibility (FLEK-suh-buhl-ih-tee)—the ability to bend or move easily

meet (MEET)—a gymnastics competition that features many events

mount (MOWNT)—to get up on the balance beam or other gymnastics apparatus

routine (roo-TEEN)—a combination of skills performed in a gymnastics event

spotter (SPOT-uhr)—a person who keeps watch to help prevent injury

visualization (vizh-oo-uh-li-ZAY-shunn)—the act of imagining or forming a mental picture

READ MORE

Carmichael, L.E. *The Science Behind Gymnastics*. Science of the Summer Olympics. North Mankato: Capstone Press, 2016.

Savage, Jeff. *Top 25 Gymnastics Skills, Tips, and Tricks*. Top 25 Sports Skills, Tips, and Tricks. Berkeley Heights, N.J.: Enslow Publishers, 2012.

Schlegel, Elfi, and Claire Ross Dunn. *The Gymnastics Book: The Young Performer's Guide to Gymnastics*. Buffalo, N.Y.: Firefly Books, 2012.

INTERNET SITES

FactHound offers a safe, fun way to find Internet sites related to this book. All of the sites on FactHound have been researched by our staff.

Here's all you do:

Visit *www.facthound.com*

Type in this code: 9781515722229

Super-cool stuff! Check out projects, games and lots more at **www.capstonekids.com**

INDEX